THE BEST OF A BAD SITUATION

Jamie Thrasivoulou

THE BEST OF A BAD SITUATION

BY JAMIE THRASIVOULOU

©Jamie Thrasivoulou, 2017
Design by Hristo Dochev
Edited by Adam Steiner and Raef Boylan

Published in the UK (2017)
by Silhouette Press

COVENTRY-LONDON

www.silhouettepress.co.uk
@SilhouettePress

ISBN 9780993431531

For Faye & Jessica

MADE IN DERBY

Contents

But

     the HEAD is fuzzed,
     the body, rigid:
your walk
     is like
   a unique
      hybrid, moving between
C-3P0 and John Wayne,
       a bicycled-copper breezes by—
says hello,
   you respond, despondently
         although you'd rather not at all.
the mind is:
       a bombastic chasm
      waiting on self-destruction,
from which
you can
reference insanity
whenever required:

it flows smooth
       like Shakespeare sonnets,
but
   less monotonous.
        the ATMOSPHERE
   is cramped
but   the SPACE is open
to interpretation—
opinion divided,
but given by every man, woman and unicorn
         mode set to survival
but— you see doubt beyond the horizon,
        feel its grip, burnt by rage,
just, what, is this?
     You-have-spoken,
to everybody
   In the room—
except one:

But—
    you do,
            make —
eye contact.

Common Sewerage Problem

Start life in terraced houses; end up dead in one.

Like packs of rabbits STACKED, heads numbed, crushed

by jaws of ravenous dogs,

Lack of movement enabled, feeds uninhibited sex drives.

They all fall down:

Everyone, everywhere; all due to their own mis-invention:

Not everyone is born a rocket scientist.

Mental is everyone outspoken and equally devoted to speaking their minds,

Seek retribution in confession;

Come fornicate with your local, disloyal priest,

Kiss the feet of Jesus for he loves you.

Change the channel for the commercial break:

Signals beamed through satellites- all converge to form the same lies—

Swallowed and shat-out in rugged, municipal vines:

Everything is done for the prosperity of the common person—

Diversion tactics employed by tactile puppets on Illuminati strings:

To be pulled whenever they please,

Common bleeds the sense,

To drip,

Then trickle,

Down to the sewers:

All to flow one way: Beneath the feet of power

That Pebbledash Finish

Distinctly working-class in every way
Though I've never celebrated St. George's day
Distinctly working-class in every way
That's right: I educated myself beyond the Patron Saint

Distinctly working-class in every way
A pebbledash finish since my birth-date
Distinctly working-class in every way
Not a day goes by without the stress of money

Distinctly working-class in every way
That's why most my life I took baths instead a' showers,
Spent hours memorizing verse whilst you've
Spent hours memorizing Latin-horticultural terms (but, then, what's the
difference?)

Distinctly working-class every day of my life
Even when I educated myself despite your advice
So what now, now I gotta' degree?
Like anyone takes that seriously:
Particularly, when your postcode begins *D-E*

Distinctly working-class in every way
There ain't many who can say that genuinely in this language game
Distinctly working-class in every way
File next to Leonard, Welsh, Kelman & Harrison

But don't take that for arrogance; it's just
That, much the same, I hold the consensus that
My voice mustn't remain confined or restricted by a categorical mistake,
        Just because I've only existed – correction: *survived and thrived* –
        more than subsisted – in the lower echelons of this
Classist-system, trapped in the race towards worst place.

I'm distinctly working-class in every way
The scars, the crooked teeth, harsh-sandpapered-skin
I'm distinctly working-class in every way

A blemish on your literary-landscape
I'm distinctly working-class in every way
    That pebbledash finish,
    Seems like you work at it, every day –
THAT PEBBLEDASH FINISH!
That just won't go away,

The Reformed Economist

You were the man about town: enticing deadbeats to hunt-you-down,
To score them Pills, or bottles of Ket, Reams of Acid-Tabs, Nine-bars of Phet,

It was anything-possible: everything had a market-price and hook-line-sinker potential clientele,
Delivered from hand-to-mouth from rented cars, or prescribed by scallies in dodgy-bars,

Your life was not your own but you always held the key, to unlock the constant chemical tapestry, ignorant to the risk of spending life at the pleasure of her Majesty,

Like Spud; your pleasure, *was other people's leisure,*
A measured glance, directed wrong, was normally received—only amidst the stench of weed,

Your confidence was elemental, the ego, brash and temperamental.
Guided by hot-knives, mirrors, and double-parked lines of Ching—

At one point you could be known to have a phone for each market: The Drug King—This way it was easy to build-up a decent-size clientele, keeping busy, each line – Occupied

By the time you got annoyed with the customers chatting to everyone about where they got their drugs from— you could sell the business on, without registration papers, and all for a nice fee,

You were doing wonders by creating startup-business opportunities for the local community—Oh, back in the day, when drugs were merely a commodity,

The dull familiarity of un-sensed sounds, vagrant frowns, (and) countless clowns of kinship, bulging-eyes, gulping-gullets: choking on internal dialogue

Which by the end of the night would end up external: particularly if the conversation one-had-with-oneself were debased in content,

In a world of faceless disease you found your place to be useful, youthful, and truly truthful, you shared the love equally: did your bit for the big bad society

Monsieur Hammond and Madame May could learn a lot from geezers like *you*—on how to boost the economy.

A True Liar

A true *liar* is:
Someone who lies to themselves,
Or so I've always been taught,

I lie to myself,
All the time
But I'll always lie to myself
Before I'd ever lie to you.

So does that make me:

A) A good liar

B) A bad liar

Or

C) A true liar?

 Let the jury hang a while,
 They're taking their time to decide.

Options

it seems that I must
de-educate myself
in order to make
a living

stop trying to
be too profound
exhaust every statement:
write scripts for contrived

telly soaps
that require
nothing other
than the

continued
suspension of
    disbelief
      dreams of the earth
      that never get off the ground

the odd person
rising-from-the-dead
will do you no harm

keep the plot brief,
story-line, thin
cheap and tacky
with a serious
undertone – a wound that sticks

and never,
ever forget
the *brand* and
what it is trying
to achieve:
C-O-M-P-L-E-T-E
      Control

Anxiety Pipped Me to the Finish Line...

Turn left at the haberdashery; keep on the path to the right-hand side.
Take the next right down chicken-clock-crescent and get on the air-ferry to
Gloucester. Pick up the mushrooms and run for the train,
through fields of green veneer, growing weed-type plants of pollen.
Sneeze *a-tissue*;

You can feel it – gripped by your everlasting anxiousness.

A gorge the size of Cheddar threatens to swallow you whole
where scare-crows scare men and women only; crows and children are
entertained and laugh at the sight of stick-men wrapped in fluorescent worker
jackets. Guarding cabbages and radishes and tomatoes, along with the secret
Ganja plants growing in thousands of allotments. It could be anywhere in the
country. The demographic consequences are felt North, East, South, West and
central to your inebriate soul. Exchange ignorance for gold, so you can be
sized-up by fat-cats that live in distant mansions and practice looking down
their noses in ten-grand-crystallized-mirrors underneath matching chandeliers.
Thousands stacked against you, a brick wall of bills, life throws cards to take in
and harbour as victims of tragedy rambunctious in disaster. The ramifications
speak clearly now as the light of day- Birds chirp-chirping; A new morning;
Fresh-start, clean- conscience, please tick all of the above.

A glimmer of hope in the dilated eyes; need a corner-shop; not a *brimful of
Asha* on the forty-five but a can of Red Stripe for the long walk home; harassed
by strangers, diverted from thought, lost in hope of obtaining a lighter for a
cigarette;
And do you, by any chance, have a spare one?

Then collapsing, and breaking down in public; like a child, floor-sprawled and shaking: your nervous disposition finally getting the better of you. Anxiety is the winner as they kick and pound at your head and ribs and your nose that's smashed into shards of flesh and bone and the pockets that are being rumbled; phone and money taken, knife to your throat as they slip the keys from your pocket – *Where do you fucking live, cunt?* And the shaking, and the nervousness, all the while stopping you talking, holding your throat; then one of them looking slightly remorseful and confronting all of the others, stopping them from hurting you and then getting on the ground and hugging you and stroking your hair in an overly-friendly way. Waking on the bathroom floor and realising it's over, and that a stranger can become a friend; particularly when you find yourself the victim of a bad acid trip

Steve Slash & the RDT

Monday morning: 9:15, late to work and far from clean,
Back from a weekend away at the football: *living the dream*

I'm reiterating tales of numerous routes and other people's coups
When our-boy, Tommy enters: puss like sour cream

Listen, Stevie yer wanna pipe down, there's deffo a grass in this workhouse
Office-Tasha, just warned us there's a bunch of testers heading straight for us

My eyes bulge, my belly-acid boils, the palpitations chemically inaugural:
No fuckin' way, random drugs test on a fuckin' Monday?

A lot of the lads' faces completely lose their complexion
But being a keen fighter Stevie always carries protection:

I've gotta screwdriver if they need readjustin'
'N' a Rubber-Johnny if they needer good fuckin'

I pull my wallet from my pocket and beckon over Tommy,
Passing him the Johnny and a twenty-sheet, discreetly

I tell him: *fill it fuller piss 'n' I'll forever hold you in the highest:*
Come on Tom I'm 10% man and 90% drugs: without you I'm fuckt!

> Good old Tommy gets off to the bogs and comes back brandishing a
> Costa coffee cup; *bought yer a brew mate* he says: grin-pinned across his
> face,

When the test-tube bastards eventually arrive I'm fired-up
I've already taken the Johnny from the cup and placed it down my sock,

Walking cautiously, I'm the first one to the bogs,
A screw-face looks us up and down: passes me a pot,

In the cramped-cubicle I get my foot up on the seat,
Removing the Johnny delicately, I hold it: gentle-as-can-be

I gag as I bite the nib, as Tommy's piss enters my lips,
Then drips, nicely into the pot: still feeling realistically hot,

I wash my hands; water my face, leaving the toilets with less than disgrace
The only trace of evidence: a piss-soaked rubber in my pocket

I deposit the sample and head for the canteen where our-boy Tommy's waiting,
Seemingly, with a speech in mind, asking— *when am I gonna stop this life?*

All, in good time, I tell him, winking, pumping with adrenaline, as I consider my
options for the evening

Hibernation

The Apple snarls, eyeballing me- its evil glare outshining the lamplight
        Nature scares beyond rectification, scars, numbs, pulls
        numb nerves with pliers,
Another time, another place, we'd sleep well,
  Now I can't relax for the buzz of satellites and government spies in jumbo jets
        that glide like birds over our sleepy city.
Secret bases in countryside landscapes of all shapes and sizes
  No doubt soon to be deformed in appearance due to military testing- we only
        got so much land: this ain't America you know!

    Worms hibernate in soil constantly, well, kind of, although science might
disagree.
        Sometimes, you gotta look deep down to find the problem.

Trouble is, people choose to play blind – forget the lost art of interrogation,
accept the lamest of lazy answers.
  I'm more concerned with the lack of Imagination; everybody's too intoxicated,
        stuck with the garbage
        on the box,
Play it down, keep it cool, stay real; attack verbally and arm yourselves with
glorious syntax —
 avoid staying in control, at all times.

Reflections

Don't nod
Madam
—Top spot—
                              ?was it a cat I saw?
:Step on no pets:
:Sagas:
No lemon, no melon
A nut for a jar of tuna
Red rum, sir, is murder
:Bird rib:
Boob
        Rotator
Golf? No sir, prefer prison flog
                    ?Eva, can I see bees in a cave?
        ?I did, did I?
Rats at a bar grab at a star
:Refer:
:Rats paraded a rap star:
                      ?Rats Paraded a rap star?
Test tube: but set
Tube debut
Too bad I hit a boot
Flee to me: remote elf
                  !Elk rap song? No sparkle!
Evil, a sin is alive
Boob
        :Radar:
Elite title
Tons o' snot
Draw nine men inward
Party booby-trap
Poor Dan is in a droop
Maps, DNA and spam
Mr. owl ate my metal worm
Level
                  I'm a pup am I?
    God's dog

God lived as a devil dog
:God saw I was a dog:
:Goddamn Mad-dog:

Anywhere Street, DE1

Tarmac roads of quicksand effect
    Six-foot fences, to cage us in
    rabbit-traps for
Destitute houses.
    Shops to let — don't look like letting
    Anyone in
    Diamonds cut the earth
    Broken glass shining dog shit
Replaces the ground beneath my feet.
Gang-tags sprayed-across street-signs,
Demonstrate the lost direction of youth:
Alienated by society,
And quite possibly let down by their Mam and Dad.
Education begins at home,
But some of these cats 'bin left to roam since the day dot,
Huddled 'round corner-shops
Givin' it the *BLAT-BLAT-BLAT*

    The same place where habitual whine-drinkers
    Gather about glass hands
To trade intoxicated philosophies
With their brothers and sisters
Of smacked-up, gouched-out descent,
The gurning speed-freak says his piece too;
Face contorted, tongue twisted,
Chewin-onner-bagger-spanners
Sammy stumbles over—
Passes the Dutch 'pon the right-hand side,
But they let *'im-off*
After all, he's steam-boated:
It's two in the afternoon fer God's sake-
The man's bin onnit fer 'ours—Whatter legend!

    As I observe this play-out
    From kerb to eye
It feeds and starves the hungry mind,
Where yer mother, nature, is nowhere in sight.

On Tag

Hosepipe the cobbles

        Thirty-six minutes to go before G4S ring the phone

Naked fences, display scuffed fibres of un-loved flesh

            Roof-tiles, missing teeth

Decayed door, rotten exits

      The letter 'W' from a keyboard – misspelt amongst pebbles

           Sweep the fag-nubs

           after their fog

        Still frosting-up the windowsill

But first—

Dust them for lipstick and fingerprints: remove the dead leaves

        Of poison Ivy that grows anonymously

Around a Ladder's metallic skeleton,

Scabbed with rust.

           Dog shit –

          Smells like evidence

Ripened, unadulterated, ammonia waves invisibly—

      The rat trapped in the cage at the end of the garden—

      The kind no clever man would ever choose to set free.

The Best of a Bad Situation

I

three weeks later and the hospital-monitor
beeps me awake from sleep
all the movement
is trapped: nothing; numbed under nothing, and nauseated stillness.
what happened after?
after what? a buzzer? a bang! must be a buzzer,
but the thoughts don't bring nothing; thoughts do not equal
movement, motion
       and a buzzer – just humming. to reach a buzzer on the wall?
       nurse, nurse? doctor? i'm here,
i'm back,
here, back on my back
but the voice weak, hear myself think…
without the buzzer – how to hear, to hear-speak?

broken equation, deleted/erased, all in error,
surely an error equals zero?
and the eyes, adjusting to the constant light, avoiding the bright
lips feel chapped and crackling, blood kissing
the sheets, white, white, not-quite-perfect white, NHS Standard
i am here, no doubting that, but all doubt
and pain? plenty of none, but feeling neither, not pain or nothing.
nurse? doctor? buzzer? movement? brain and limbs
connect? what's converse?
the dichotomy of my body taking its place?
blank blips – to monitor nothing – a nothing monitor…

and when they enter, to tell you
what you already
know:
       no more windmills
       from the waist, down.

II

They come every day now
Various nurses, carers – interchangeable.
Today, when she arrives,
The Jamaican lass,
I'm crashed out
On the bloody bed
    Spliff still hanging
    Half in and out my mouth
I am what's stinking the
Bloody place out:
    Imagine that?
    I don't have to, because
This is reality—ha-ha
I apologise, or try to, but she,
Politely declines it.
Says it's 'My choice' what I do
She won't be callin'
The police, which is
Okay then. I guess.
She must think different things
    Of me, at different times,
    'Cause the other day I
Told her to go away.
I was still hungover, but
She didn't look offended
Like she was expecting it,
Like she's already heard
From the others *what I'm like*
But I don't really mind that
    Because they are all nice,
    In their different ways.

In fact, they are all bloody great
Imagine having their job - shoving enemas up people's arses all day?
I mean they all seem to be women, too so it can't be nice
A man's arse – several times a day?
Jesus wept.

They've kept me going, I suppose
Keeps you on your toes, having visitors,
In my case, of course, in the proverbial sense.
And she is soon done, dusted and gone
Which means soon it will come, and I'll have to move
Either that or wait for the carer to come and clean me up

III

I pull myself up, onto the roof
     The lads are all goading me
     From
     Down
Below.
     They don't believe
     I've got the balls
     To do it.

     I strip down to my boxers and
Socks –
Fuckit,
Off with them too, I do a few
Wind-mills
With the old-boy for the lads
(And lasses)
Now gathered,
Waiting for what's next.

Admittedly, I am worse for wear
But what's a bit of flying through the air?
 I take position, one person waves
Another screams,
Waves –
Screaming, about what?
I jump, oh to jump through the humid air whilst all those pretty girls stop and
stare
then
Hitting water
     and the crunch of bones

'Cause
it is
too
     damn
     shallow
Then — Nothing:
Not even darkness/just nothing/less than a void/we cannot speak of…
Three-weeks in, the beeping starts – *the beeps repeat* – my ears follow my

heart,
   The ruffling of paper,
   The shuffling of bodies.

IV

Eight years since
The accident
Corrected me.
You might well laugh
At that,
But in a way it did:
It broke my body
But it fixed my mind.

     I only have one friend left
From way back when,
The rest were fair-weather
In the truest sense,
And I don't hold it against them.

To begin with, everything is difficult,
Harder to accept.
The situation:
     My pissed-up judgment, of mis-judged steps
     Ignoring the waving, screaming stupidity
That greeted my literal downfall
     But that is now over, and I
I accept the accident and I accept myself,
My deconstructed, *disabled form.*

I had let myself become everything I hated
A huge, exacerbated, wind-milling
     Cock-out, cocky fucker, just consuming everything; all the products,
alcohol, uppers and downers the world could throw at me.
     Nowadays, I only smoke and get pissed
     Every now and then.

Don't get me wrong:
But I've moved on
There's university (Box ticked)
Travelling to America (Box ticked)
Reading up on Mindfulness (Box ticked)
Considering religion (Box ticked)
Reaffirming religion is not for me but learning to respect it (Box ticked)

Seen way too many bands and live acts to mention (Box ticked)
Influencing a set of poems (Box ticked)
With much more to come!
     (Lots of boxes left for me to tick)
     Both positive and negative.

Now:
My cock don't work but my mind does
My cock don't work but my mind does
That's what I say to everyone
It makes us laugh

Beneath a Banana Moon

Once activated
Your dark-side will always exist
It's simply a question of how much you indulge it

Or
How often
It chases you down
The never-ending stairwells of despair—
There's no magic pill for the mental my dear—

You say fear?
I say show me: Outside this head it's merely white noise

But You?
You wouldn't let knowledge or logic cloud your judgement:
So-Enlightened-Art-Thou

Stuck in ruts of dated essence
Fan-flamed building of resolute structure:
Glass blown out & Brick loose

Your silicon smile becomes visible
Through a smoldering haze

I glance both ways before passing through your shadow:
You've no foot soldiers in tow —
There's no witnesses to deal the legal blow

It's just you,
Me,
The moon & the train yard

My right hand engages with my trouser pocket,
The set of house keys gripped tight in a firm embrace:
A fistful of steel & a head full of rage

Escalating the rugged mish-mash terrain
I'm soon within range:
You look around as though expecting to be followed

I feel a sense of predatory pride
So I howl at the moon twice:
Once for Ginsberg, & once again,
For a round of fucks!

The graffiti-adorned crumbling walls are an inspiration
You-Could-Be
The final piece in this artistic puzzle:
My Adrenalin times Your Claret = Modern Art:
Now exhibiting the Shit-kicked Scum-bag!

BOOM!

My conscience breaks my stride
As I am down-lifted by the up-trodden prey I pursue

I stand still:
Slack-gobbed,
Remorseful
Devoid of facial expression

As you approach the mattress underneath the street light
The same one I pissed on last night:
You flip it onto the footpath
& Sit down cross-legged

I hang-about in the shadows on tiptoes
As you roll up your sleeve to reveal
Tracked & Tested territory

I witness your defeated soul in full bloom
As the sparks collide with the silver-spoon
Hypodermic: Locked & Loaded:
As you fire,
That fatal shot
Beneath the thrown
Banana moon

Duck

Bluebells bash Tulip-tops
As they battle
For the cover of Conifers.

The Beetles, Ants, and other crawlies,
Anticipating rain,
        Made a ready home
        From the nearest hole.

Time ter get the washin' in then, duck
The Mrs. says,
Poking me with the peg-basket.

Raw Fish vs. Cooked Fish

My eardrums feel perforated
    By the syncopated squawks
    Of gulls,
Nowhere near the sea.
Chips and battered sausages
Dangle from their beaks,
Couples of beans and pairs of mushy peas cling,

Man…this is the life

So, I think - they think – FEED ME
As they perch above their third
Free-meal of the day
It sure beats hanging-out-at-sea,
At least around here the food's cooked!

I suppose it must be a nightmare—
For a seagull
    To try and light the oven
    Out at sea

Anthem For the Racist White Trash

It's every day it's 5AM
I'm out walking the dogs again
On the corner of my street whom should I see?
But local people, both immigrants and refugees

You say:
They're queuing to take those jobs you dream
They're queuing to take those jobs you dream

Of packing chickens in factories
Or wiping the arses of amputees
Exploited loyal worker bees
Half their wages docked for travel fees

They're here to steal those jobs you dream
They're here to steal those jobs you dream

Like picking strawberries from the fields
Bent down cramped-up and on their knees
Or washing cars for a fiver-a-piece
Or saving the NHS that's on its knees

They're here to steal those jobs you seek
They're here to steal those jobs you seek

Like flipping horsemeat-burgers at the football
Or cleaning the greasy tables in food-halls
Sweeping the tarmac, picking-up the litter
you drop on our streets

They're here to steal those jobs you seek
They're here to steal those jobs you seek

Like stacking the shelves of your local Tesco
Or arranging the bouquet which adorns your window

Serving you Donner meat when you're half-baked
Manning the underground day-by-day
For better-off tourists, bankers, and ignorant oligarchs
Or serving your McDonald's hangover breakfasts
Plastic-coffee-cup, pancake-pot, radioactive bacon rolls:
Whilst you English White-Trash sit and stay at home;
death by daytime telly, lapping-up your dole,

They're here to steal those jobs you pretend to seek
They're here to steal those jobs you pretend to seek
They're here to steal those jobs, that you — wouldn't wanna do

Won't Turn to Dust

Our art will always prevail,
It's better than the entrails
Of life we are fed from birth:

Work chides
Our arctic soul;
Free thought, forgotten courage.

This is evidenced
By the dummies placed in our
Mouths to stop us whining

To the dummies we become;
  Our dummy government
  Pacified in absence

Keeping our art in hiding
Whilst they debate around
The tables *we* helped pay for

On how best to waste what-was *our* cash
At in-between times
Times of peace during war

  There's only one thing we should say
About ourselves:
Our words will always prevail
They won't just turn to dust
Waiting on the shelf

Dead Letters

To the
Postbox I went
Letters
Proudly on
Show
But when I reached
The corner there was
No red in view
Just the flashing blue of
A cop-van and a few
Loose letters strewn:
Lost songs blowing in the wind

I asked the copper: where's the
Box?
He looked us up-and-down
All sussed out.
Now then laddie, what can you tell
Me about this?
I held up my letters in defence:
Come on, man – I need to get this form in
Fer me Mam's rent, but it was no use,
The copper took my defence for abuse;
he didn't need to pull his truncheon out
To make a display of my rights.
He told me to jog-on,
I'd be cautioned this time,
But he'd got my number.

It shook me up fair, it did.
So I went up the road, near the church,
And used that postbox instead.

When I told Uncle Stevie about our postbox he just laughed,
And started ranting:

It probably won't get replaced, either: being as the council spent
That much money on their council house refurb:
We'll be lucky to get one of those red tin-boxes,
Them that look more like a fuckin' bin than a postbox.
Never mind one of yer old pillar ones.
And so far he's right,
We haven't even got the tinny-bin job:
The council just filled the hole in.

Who's der Clevrist Man Yer Know?

I-knock-the-door and Weston answers

Come in breddeh we Listnin' Inter Pirate station
Wi-record las' week
        Who's der clevrist man yer know who ever lived?
Dem Steven Hawkin right?
 I shrug,
I s'poze he's up there?

Man here talk 'bout Haile Selassie
Clev'rist man who ever walk d' eart ya see now, me fren
More PHD's and honourary letters afteriz name
than letters of dem alphabet

Fuckin' whitewashed mainstream press always be talkin
like Steven Hawkin' dee-clevrist man on de eart
or sumtin;
man 'pon wheelchair speakin tru computer?

SSHHMMUUUUTTTT (KISS-DE-TEET-SOUND)

Fuckin' bullshit man,
No man who speak
Tru computer's der true righteous holly warrior:
Haile Selassie: more letters dan dem alphabet
Get ter fuck widjer raceest bullsheet
Whiteman always gotta be dem celvrist:
Fuck yer Steven Hawkin'

I might have worded it differently myself but
I could see Weston's point: Haile Selassie
Was hardly mentioned in popular history:
He undoubtedly should be, without this man
We'd have no peace and unity on earth at all.

I passed Weston the joint and he switched the amp
From auxiliary to phono, placed the needle down:
Zion's Blood from *Super-Ape* vibrated the room,
African blood is present in all of us.

Hunting Snow in a Blizzard

Dodging the glances of former friends,
    Pretending not to know, you know anyone.
    Waiting on a chance to enter the wings,
The security guard has already clocked
That I'm not really lookin' to *buy* from this shop.

    A casual check of the watch: He inspects me, inspecting some stock.
I Eye-up the aisles for items untagged:
Check the Cameras for black spots,
Info gathered – I leave the shop

I take a slow walk-around the shopping-block
Aware that lunchtime will soon be prime
The security guard will soon be tucking into a Bird's cob –
The perfect time to commit the crime.

On a come-down I'm starting to writhe around,
I need the proper-bad goods to secure my fix
A few o' them Yankee-candles ought to do the trick
Route diverted, a cash-desk left untended

I run through the door and grab a wad of tokens
No cash in sight: hardly worth my plight
What's more it's probably brought it all on top,
I've got to get-gone: I exit shop-right and scram.

Like my life is in slow motion
My mind a void emotion,
Brimming with the hope of the next raise
That I hope will pay the drug debts, forgotten yesterday

I need that snowball hit to get me fixed
Or I'm gonna start shaking in public
I return to the store where the coast is clear
No security twat around to interfere

I liberate the goods in the sincerest of fashion
And head straight outta town to portion my rations
To the good old people of the local boozer,
Most of which have me down as a loser

As I enter with pockets full of candles,
One bloke says I look a shambles
But he can't handle the fact I make a living from this
Whilst he just sits around and gets pissed,
With the goods sold, I'm over the road
Placing coins in the phone-box
When from outta nowhere the cop-car pulls up

Some fuckin' cunt in the pub has grassed-us-up
But the goods are long gone, so I carry on
Making the call for the snowball,
I arrange the meet on Abbey Street

Prepared to be lifted from my feet by the copper
Who unsurprisingly wants to search my pockets:
'Cause he's heard I've been *shopping again,*
Although he already *knows* he won't find-a-thing

We go through the process I answer their questions
Sign the sheet and get off in time to score my bits
I meet my dealer outside the derelict takeaway
We do-the-deal
Bid farewell
And that is me — fixed

Feeling the Burn

society dictates
that big business
pays low rates
whilst the working class
are treated like
a HATE crime
waiting everyday
for home time
watching—
the tick-tocking
of clocks,
which are deliberately
set-back
five minutes
to make
you work longer.

the one positive
aspect of this
charitable work
is that
it gives you
more time
to think about
when
it
will
all
just
burn
out
for
good

About That Postbox...

I borrowed the van with the big bull-bars
From work
No way I was letting that letter
Get there:
Me Mam ticked the wrong box on the
Disability form
Which means: 'A change of circumstance'
Which means stopping the benefit
            Which means getting fuck all –
She can't afford that.
But those council fuckers
Can definitely afford
A new postbox
So that's what it had to be!
Fuck 'em.

Reimagining Yeroskipou

If I trotted back to
Village streets dragging feet of
Dust-fetched plumes

Who would notice
My face of visitor's concern
On sun-engraved veranda

Two decades ago we sat:
My family-tree woven from people, generations
Bloomed from Cypriot-blood

Trans-fused via Britain:
Would that same family
Living in my memory,

To replace my family's fractured tree,
Recognize my vine-like reach?
Sprawled-out-in-a-Datsun-hot-seat

Windows down, roof hatched-back
And relishing the salacious Cypriot sun
A time, when I had two homes encases my mind

Yearning for a flashback of untainted tears
Gained from sour-sharp limes and nectarines,
Burned flesh from Spatchcocked chickens

Portions of Souvlaki: *endaxi ray*
Ella, ella ray: Papou's persuasive
Tongue echoes from the disused grill

The shutters on the window cascade shadows
Closedown the cancerous room,
Shrink the deathbed where leukemia held him hostage

The nights and days drew thin
As his disheveled skin, skeletal in comparison
To the stature of a man

Whose image remains untainted, still smiling
Don't let night or dark fool you Papou:
For your memory ascends, far beyond these walls

The Old Enemy

In your youth it used to guide you/over the cast-iron cellar-grates of terraced houses/it would kick stones and bits of rubbish down the holes and gaps— filling blackness

It would even let your dog piss over them/No quarter or consideration given/ to the total desecration of another human's dwelling/

You could often be found staggering around back-alleys/Tripping over cobbled-stones/Crouched behind industrial bins having a cheeky line or bangin' Some bird you'd barely just met/and sometimes both at the same time/

Stumbling from casinos, leaving wasted cappuccinos on the side/Most of the time down-on-luck/full of fucks and other curses (but none to give) /sanity long deserted/Time, please/long-past closing/

But once you were in for the win/A wedge of pink-crisp notes – over five grand/A stunner had attached herself to your arm for the night/Claimed she was your lucky charm, here to aid your plight/Let's take the house down together, darling/She told you that: You were real charming: just the type-of-guy she was always looking for/The rendezvous was planned for afterhours/

Now it's after that/but you think she's more like: after YOURS/As in money/ She is keeping bad company/but that's the attraction/The danger element/ She leads you away/in self-pursuit/Complete with wannabe hard-man in a cheap Gangster suit/You'd already heard him sniffing in the loos/needing more than booze to cruise for the bruise/ Not even a has-been/more like a never was/But nevertheless, he looked a keen tryer

About your heels, like a rat/Chemical-carnage spread across his chops as you smash his face into the shutters of Greggs – the pasty shop/As he flops to the floor/The sound of an opening door/taxi driver getting out/Fuck that, get back in/You urge him/You leave the woman cursing at the fellow who's still crouched into a ball/Must be winded bad/Not your fault, on this occasion/but night's like this will always reaffirm/That the ego/is an old enemy/ best left in the past, to burn/

The Blemish

I am part of the final polish that lifts the tone,
As light reflects - collecting the insects in passing
The missing tile above the fireplace
That is, painted over, instead of being replaced.

The rough finish disfiguring
Your final version,
Nothing worse than a blemish
To make one's work seem less-than-perfect.
Why take the time to sand and grind away
Half a century's paint, just to leave it looking rubbish?

To hell with it, the customer is right, what they say sits best,
You are paid to take it, better than not being paid at all.
But surely a blemish of blobs, smothered in gloss, is grossly uncalled for?
To my mind's eye the job ought to be done *pro-per-l-y* – or not at all.

But just what is an eye in the mind?
More like pies in the greedy sky!
Carry on slaving away whilst Mr. BBC blathers on through the wireless,
Your mask, tied tight,
You follow particles of dust, atoms colliding
With the hazy rays of sunshine
          Washing the window opaque.

Re-hang that door; whoever did it last
Not nearly enough,
Catches on the bloody carpet
Needs a good chunk planing-off
Botched jobs everywhere;
They'll be the death of me.

Jamie Thrasivoulou is a poet/spoken word artist from Derby.

By trade he is a painter and decorator – but now he mostly spends his time facilitating creative-writing workshops.

Jamie works with Asylum Seekers and Refugees for the Writing East Midlands Write Here Sanctuary project where he is shadow Writer-in-Residence.

He has published in Paper + Ink zine, Burning house press, Hand-Job-Zine, Pint Pot Poetry, The Arsonist Magazine, Cityzine, and Not-So-Popular.

Jamie runs the poetry night Word Wise in Derby, and performs all over the UK.

Jamie's website: **http://jthras.com**
@JMThras

Acknowledgements

I would like to acknowledge some of the characters and alter egos that exist in this collection. Those of you, who know who you are, have asked to remain unmentioned so this is a big thanks for inspiration in certain pieces. Without your stories some of these poems wouldn't exist. To those of you who don't know I've written about you – good luck in proving it.

Reimagining Yeroskipou was previously published by *Burning House Press*

On Tag & Anywhere Street DE1 were previously published in *The Arsonist Magazine*

The Old Enemy was previously published by *Hand-Job-Zine*

There is Reference to the character *Spud* from the film adaptation of *Trainspotting* in *The Reformed Economist*

I'd like to give a massive shout out to friends and family for your continued support in life. Particularly the following Creatives: Everyone @ Silhouette Press (Adam, Raef, Stephen) Aimee & Henderson @ Writing East Midlands, Sophie Sparham, Rhythmical Mike, Miggy Angel, Kevin Fegan, Trevor Wright, Pr@xis, Baby J, Alex Blood, Bret James, Martin Ridgeway, Johnny Swinhoe, Antony Owen, Jim Mortram, Richard C. Bower, Daron Carey, Joe Coghlan, Steven Battelle, Cullen Marshall, Mark Theory, Keith Ford, Jim Gibson, Sophie Pitchford, Helen Mort, Matt McAteer, Martin Illingworth, Andy Graves, Jay Dean, Trevor Wright, Carl Tighe, Moy Mccrory, Simon Heywood, Matt Clegg, Chris Twarog, Micky Sheehan, Martin Appleby, Sarah Lay, Storge Music, Louder Than War, Matt Abbott, Toria Garbutt & Louise Fazackerley (Nymphs + Thugs Crew) Les Baynton & the Deda poets crew, The Twisted Tongues crew, & Anybody who has ever put me on at a gig!

But most importantly – I'd like to thank *you* for buying this book.